Ministry of Planning
Kurdistan Regional Government

Building the Future

Summary of Four Studies to Develop the Private Sector, Education, Health Care, and Data for Decisionmaking for the Kurdistan Region—Iraq

Sponsored by the Kurdistan Regional Government

RAND
CORPORATION

C. Ross Anthony
Michael L. Hansen
Krishna B. Kumar
Howard J. Shatz
Georges Vernez

For more information on this publication, visit www.rand.org/t/mg1185z2

Library of Congress Cataloging-in-Publication Data is available for this publication.

ISBN: 978-0-8330-9311-0

Published by the RAND Corporation, Santa Monica, Calif.

© Copyright 2016 Kurdistan Regional Government

RAND® is a registered trademark.

Cover images used with permission. Background image courtesy of Howard J. Shatz. Porthole images (left to right) courtesy of Howard J. Shatz, the RAND Corporation, Superstock, and iStockphoto.

Support RAND
Make a tax-deductible charitable contribution at
www.rand.org/giving/contribute

www.rand.org

Preface

In 2010, Dr. Ali Sindi, Minister of Planning, on behalf of the the Kurdistan Regional Government (KRG), asked the RAND Corporation to undertake four studies aimed at improving the economic and social development of the Kurdistan Region—Iraq (KRI). RAND's work was intended to help the KRG expand access to high-quality education and health care, increase private-sector development and employment for the expanding labor force, and design a data-collection system to support high-priority policies. The studies were carried out over the year beginning February 2010. The RAND teams worked closely with the Ministries of Planning, Education, and Health to develop targeted solutions to the critical issues faced by the KRG.

This document summarizes the four studies, the detailed findings of which have been published in four separate reports. It is intended to provide a high-level overview of the approaches followed by the studies and their key findings and major recommendations. We expect this summary document to be of interest to policymakers in the KRG, as well as a broad audience concerned with social and economic reform in the KRI.

The four individual studies are documented in the following reports:

- Michael L. Hansen, Howard J. Shatz, Louay Constant, Alexandria C. Smith, Krishna B. Kumar, Heather Krull, Artur Usanov, with Harun Dogo, Jeffrey Martini, *Strategies for Private-Sector Development and Civil-Service Reform in the Kurdistan Region—Iraq*, Santa Monica, Calif.: RAND Corporation, MG-1117-KRG, forthcoming
- Georges Vernez, Shelly Culbertson, Louay Constant, *Strategic Priorities for Improving Access to Quality Education in the Kurdistan Region—Iraq*, Santa Monica, Calif.: RAND Corporation, MG-1140-KRG, forthcoming
- Melinda Moore, C. Ross Anthony, Yee-Wei Lim, Spencer S. Jones, Adrian Overton, Joanne K. Yoong, *The Future of Health Care in the Kurdistan Region—Iraq: Toward an Effective, High-Quality System with an Emphasis on Primary Care*, Santa Monica, Calif.: RAND Corporation, MG-1148-KRG, forthcoming
- Sandra H. Berry, Nicholas Burger, Harun Dogo, Krishna B. Kumar, Alessandro Malchiodi, Jeffrey Martini, Tewodaj Mengistu, Howard J. Shatz, Alexandria C. Smith, Artur Usanov, Joanne Yoong, *Designing a System for Collecting Policy-Relevant Data for the Kurdistan Region—Iraq*, Santa Monica, Calif.: RAND Corporation, MG-1184-KRG, forthcoming.

The research documented in these reports and summarized in this volume was sponsored by the KRG and conducted by the RAND Corporation. For more information about the studies or about the RAND Corporation, please contact Robin Meili, director of International

Programs, by email at Robin_Meili@rand.org, by phone at +1-310-393-0411 extension 7190, or by mail at the RAND Corporation, 1776 Main Street, P.O. Box 2138, Santa Monica, CA 90407-2138. More information about RAND is available at www.rand.org.

Contents

CHAPTER FOUR
The Future of Health Care in the Kurdistan Region—Iraq 17

CHAPTER FIVE
**Developing a System for Collecting Policy-Relevant Data for the Kurdistan
    Region—Iraq** 27

CHAPTER SIX
Summary and Conclusion 41

Figure and Tables

Figure

Tables

Acknowledgments

We are grateful to the KRG for supporting this research. We are particularly indebted to the generous sponsorship, guidance, and assistance of His Excellency Dr. Ali Sindi, Minister of Planning. We also thank His Excellency Dr. Taher Abdullah Hawrami, Minister of Health; and His Excellency Safeen Mohsin Dizayee, Minister of Education. Within the Ministry of Planning, we thank Mr. Zagros Fatah Siwaily, the Director General of Development Coordination and Cooperation, who provided invaluable guidance and facilitation, and Mr. Serwan Mohamed, head of the Kurdistan Region Statistics Office (KRSO), for providing us with data from the KRSO. Dr. Amer Omar within the Ministry of Health and Ms. Parzheen Abdulrahman Ali and Ms. Dastan Abdulrahman Ali within the Ministry of Education provided critical assistance throughout the duration of the studies. We also thank the staff of each of the Planning, Health, and Education ministries, who were exceedingly generous with their time and support of our efforts. Hundreds of people throughout the region graciously gave their time, shared their ideas, candidly answered the many questions we had, and provided data during the course of the studies. We also thank those within the government who assisted us with advice, translation, and transportation; this study would not have been successful without their tireless efforts.

Abbreviations

COSIT	Central Organization for Statistics and Information Technology
CQI	continuous quality improvement
DIM	Department of Information and Mapping
DoIT	Department of Information Technology
DPT	diphtheria-pertussis-tetanus
GIS	geographic information system
IHSES	Iraq Household Socio-Economic Survey
ICT	information and communications technology
IT	information technology
KRG	Kurdistan Regional Government
KRI	Kurdistan Region—Iraq
KRSO	Kurdistan Region Statistics Office
MOP	Ministry of Planning
OECD	Organisation for Economic Co-operation and Development
PHC	primary health care center
WHO	World Health Organization

CHAPTER ONE

Introduction

Background

The Kurdistan Region—Iraq (KRI) is a semi-autonomous region of Iraq situated in the northern part of the country, bordering Iran to the east, Turkey to the north, and Syria to the west. Its area is similar in size to that of the Netherlands and Switzerland. The establishment of the KRI dates back to March 1970, when an autonomy agreement was signed between the Kurdish opposition and the Iraqi government after years of heavy fighting, but the current incarnation gets its authority from the post-Saddam Iraqi constitution that provides for regions within Iraq. The KRI is divided into three governorates: Duhok, Erbil, and Sulaimaniyah. The population is thought to be around 5 million[1] and is very young, with about 50 percent under 20 years old.[2]

The KRI economy is dominated by the government sector, the oil industry, construction, and services, with agriculture and tourism gaining share. The relative security and stability of the region have allowed the Kurdistan Regional Government (KRG) to improve regional infrastructure and services to its population. The overall policy direction of the KRG is the development of a diversified economy, not dependent solely on oil, with a thriving private sector, sufficient government and social services, and an education system and labor market opportunities that will improve the standard of living for the people of the Kurdistan Region.

Methods

The four studies summarized here have employed multiple research methods. All studies conducted extensive reviews of the international literature pertaining to each field. We reviewed the laws and regulations relevant in the KRI, Iraq, and other international bodies. We conducted hundreds of interviews of ministers, government officials, civil-society organizations, and professionals in all three governorates. Throughout the region, we visited schools, colleges, and universities, where we spoke with deans, supervisors, and teachers, as well as primary care centers and hospitals, where we spoke with administrators, caregivers, and patients. A great

---

[1] The population number for the KRI is only approximate. It is based on data from Kurdistan Regional Government Ministry of Health, "MOH 2009 Annual Report," Erbil, Iraq, 2009, and an unpublished 2009 Census Frame. There has not been a recent official population census, which is the only way to get an accurate count of the population.

[2] Central Organization for Statistics and Information Technology, Kuristan Region Statistics Organization, and World Bank, "Iraq Household Socio-Economic Survey—IHSES-2007," Baghdad, Iraq, 2008. As of November 29, 2011: http://go.worldbank.org/GMS95L4VH0

deal of secondary data were analyzed, including data collected by the Kurdistan Region Statistics Office (KRSO) and the Ministries of Health and Education and data available from other organizations (for example, the World Health Organization [WHO], International Monetary Fund, World Bank, United Nations agencies, and U.S. Agency for International Development, to name a few). The health and education studies took advantage of the geographic information system (GIS) data available within the Ministry of Planning (MOP) and Ministry of Education, respectively. And finally, with the aid of the Ministry of Education, we conducted a survey of 2,904 teachers in 226 schools to assist in determining training needs for current teachers.

Organization of This Report

The remainder of this report presents summaries of each of the reports noted in the preface. Chapter Two provides strategies for the KRG to increase private-sector employment and to reemploy some civil-service workers in the private sector. Chapter Three develops strategic priorities to increase access to and the quality of basic and secondary education. Chapter Four analyzes the primary health care system in the KRI; makes detailed recommendations for improving primary care quality, access, effectiveness, and efficiency; and looks at issues of health care financing. It also offers an overview of different health insurance and health financing systems. Chapter Five outlines the policy priorities of the KRG as articulated by its officials and provides strategies for collecting data to further these priorities and recommendations for improving statistical institutions to aid collection of these data. Chapter Six provides a summary and conclusion.

CHAPTER TWO

Strategies for Private-Sector Development and Civil-Service Reform in the Kurdistan Region—Iraq

The KRG currently employs a substantial number of people working in the KRI. Indeed, of all the jobs in the region, only 20 percent are wage-paying jobs in the private sector. To ensure the long-term economic benefit of its citizens, the KRG is interested in pursuing an economic development strategy that rebalances the economy toward private-sector employment, including reemploying civil-service workers in the private sector. In this study, we analyzed the issues related to the desired economic development strategy and developed recommendations for private-sector development and both civil-service reform and downsizing.

The KRI has a very young population: About 50 percent of the population is age 20 or younger. Although some jobs will be vacated as people retire, there will soon be a large increase in the number of individuals who wish to work. Where will these people find jobs? One possible solution is government employment; however, policymakers are *already* concerned about the level of government employment. A more promising alternative is to develop a healthy and innovative private sector.

The KRG can develop its private sector by removing obstacles to starting or expanding a business, by identifying sectors for which conditions are particularly favorable for private-sector growth and supporting them, and by outsourcing and privatizing some functions the KRG currently performs. However, private-sector growth does not guarantee that civil-service workers will leave for private-sector employment. Civil-service workers will need the qualifications necessary for private-sector jobs, and they will have to feel that the benefits of private-sector employment outweigh the benefits of civil-service employment. At the same time, as the KRG devises methods for encouraging civil-service workers to leave for the private sector, a key challenge will be to ensure that the KRG is able to retain the employees it needs in order to ensure the proper functioning of government.

Developing the Private Sector

There are three promising, complementary strategies for private-sector development:

- domestic entrepreneurship and new business formation
- foreign direct investment
- outsourcing or privatization of government functions.

There is strong evidence that the most rapid and sustainable path for growth involves entrepreneurs and entrepreneurial firms that develop new products and services or use new methods. Encouraging local businesses is also a key element of developing an entrepreneurial economy. At the same time, foreign direct investment brings additional capital, new technologies, new management techniques and practices, and links to the global economy. Proponents of outsourcing and privatization argue that the private sector can perform many functions more efficiently and cost-effectively than governments can, easing the burden on taxpayers and freeing government resources for use on services that can benefit the whole population, such as security, education, health services, and some forms of infrastructure.

The KRI has several characteristics that make it a more favorable business environment than the rest of Iraq. Security is better; knowledgeable observers often deem the investment law to be superior to that in the rest of Iraq; and infrastructure, such as roads and electricity, already generally considered better in the KRI than in the rest of Iraq, is improving. However, there are some barriers to private-sector development, including poorly developed financial markets, difficulty acquiring land for a business, burdensome and costly procedures for registering a new business, numerous procedures for importing and exporting, availability of business information, and the lack of international arbitration in investment disputes.

Overall, the KRI offers a mostly favorable environment for foreign investors but a difficult environment for small, local businesses. With the right project, foreign investors can find entry into the KRI to be fairly smooth. However, the environment for creating new, small, local businesses appears to be challenging. This could be a barrier to economic development because, despite the benefits of large foreign investments, local capital formation is also extremely important to long-term growth.

Recommendations for Private-Sector Development

There are actions the KRG can pursue to strengthen its private sector.

The KRG should ease the formation of domestic businesses:

- Simplify procedures for starting formal small and medium-sized businesses.
- Start on legal reform of land titling and sale.

  Greater openness to the international economy will encourage private-sector development:

- Remove import and export licensing rules and restrictions.

  A more developed financial sector can help businesses form and grow:

- Consider having civil-servant salaries deposited directly into accounts in private banks.
- In any efforts to attract new financial service providers, target lenders that focus on small and medium-sized businesses.

  There is room for further improvement in public services:

- Move to greater cost recovery in electricity and water.

The legal environment for labor needs reform:

- In the reform of the labor law, consult international best practice—for example, by using experts from Organisation for Economic Co-operation and Development (OECD) countries, rather than regional models.
- Consider new rules for foreign workers, including workers from Arab countries, to enable better employment opportunities for nationals.
- Pending the reform of the pension law, enforce the payment of pension obligations by workers and companies under the current pension law.
- Continue pension reform efforts to institute a retirement system that could make private-sector employment more attractive.

Domestic and foreign businesses will find a more congenial environment if they have a fair and trusted method for settling disputes with the government:

- The KRG should explore arrangements for resolving investor disputes in an international forum.
- Over the longer term, domestic dispute resolution mechanisms, such as the courts, should be strengthened so that all businesses can settle disputes fairly, whether the disputes are with the government or other businesses.

There are some activist policies—measures that provide incentives for actions or by which the government intervenes more heavily in markets rather than just setting the rules and environment for competition—that the KRG can pursue to foster private-sector development:

- Aim investment incentives at the hiring and training of local labor, partnering with and training local businesses, and attracting industries that serve regional and global markets.
- However, additional measures beyond those incentives—specifically, requirements to use local labor or requirements to source inputs locally or take on a local partner—are likely to be counterproductive.
- Ease information barriers by collecting and making business and economic data publicly and freely available.
- Experiment with legal and regulatory reform by establishing special economic zones.

The KRG should consider two other steps designed to create a better business environment.

- Institute a modern competition law, also known as an antimonopoly law.
- Adopt a strategic plan showing a road map for policy adoption, the proposed timing, the resources necessary for accomplishing reforms, and the source of those resources.

Outsourcing and Privatization as Private-Sector Development

The KRG can also improve private-sector employment by outsourcing or privatizing. Some functions are inherently governmental; however, the private sector can perform others without compromising the ability of the KRG to serve its citizens. Furthermore, experience in other countries suggests that the private sector can often perform these functions more efficiently.

Governments outsource functions when they enter into a contract with a nongovernmental unit to provide services or carry out functions that the government would normally do itself. In contrast, privatization takes place when a state-owned enterprise or an entity within government produces goods or services usually produced by the private sector in a market economy. Full privatization is the complete sale of a state-owned enterprise to the private sector; with partial privatization, the government retains some control.

Outsourcing and privatization do not always work well. Their success often depends on the function or service being shifted to the private sector, the ability of the private sector to take on the responsibility of carrying out those functions or services, the specific contract conditions between the government and the outsourcing firm, and the government's ability to monitor. In some cases, it is better not to outsource at all. However, despite these challenges, outsourcing or privatization can move workers from the civil service to the private sector and increase the efficiency with which functions or services are performed.

Recommendations for Outsourcing and Privatization

Outsourcing. One way to outsource is to consider whether specific ministries provide services that the private sector could provide:

- In choosing what to outsource, consider ministries that provide services similar to those provided by private-sector companies.

In any single ministry, such functions likely employ only a small number of government workers. It is more likely that there are numerous workers carrying out the same functions in multiple ministries. Outsourcing those functions could result in a more substantial reduction in the size of the civil service:

- Preferably, focus on outsourcing functions within the government that are found in multiple ministries and that are also carried out by private-sector firms and workers.
- Such functions include office clerks, cleaners and launderers, motor vehicle drivers, messengers and porters, and library and mail clerks.

Deciding on functions and services to outsource will require a certain amount of knowledge about the KRG that may not now exist:

- Lay the groundwork for outsourcing by improving the KRG personnel management system—in particular, by writing job descriptions for civil servants. This will help KRG officials better identify functions to be outsourced.

These functions will still need to be performed well. Therefore, the KRG should maximize its changes of picking a good outsourcing firm:

- Ensure that tenders for outsourcing of services or functions are transparent and widely competed.

Privatization. Infrastructure is one candidate for privatization:

- Focus on sewerage and water. Although sewerage is less directly related to business development than electricity, the fact that the KRI does not have wastewater treatment plants or sewerage systems presents an immediate privatization opportunity.

- Consider privatizing additional parts of the electricity system, beyond the already-privatized generating facilities.

As with outsourcing, the KRG should maximize its chances of picking a good private-sector firm in a privatization:

- In any privatization, ensure that the process is transparent and invites competition.

The KRG has already privatized some firms, often through management contracts. If problems with these privatizations develop, there may be further opportunities for privatization:

- Reprivatize any previous privatizations that may have failed.
- Monitor the performance of the contracts under which the currently privatized entities are operating, perhaps with an independent oversight agency or a global accounting and evaluation firm, and use a transparent legal process to either encourage performance or reclaim the enterprises and then reprivatize if the contract is not being honored.

Civil-Service Downsizing and Reform

Expanding opportunities for private-sector growth does not guarantee that civil-service workers will leave government for private-sector employment or be able to obtain such employment. Private-sector employers will hire only qualified individuals they believe will be productive employees. Government employees may need training to better align their skills with those in demand in the private sector; they might also require an incentive to invest in this training.

The Ability and Qualifications of Civil Servants to Work in the Private Sector

About 20 percent of civil-service workers already work for *both* the government and private-sector employers. Furthermore, more than 90 percent of these workers have civil-service and private-sector jobs that are in different occupations. This suggests that civil-service workers can find a place in the private sector even if they cannot find jobs exactly like the civil-service jobs they now hold.

Furthermore, civil-service workers appear to be more highly skilled than current private-sector workers on at least some dimensions. This is particularly true of communication skills, which employers report they highly value. In addition, civil-service workers have higher education levels than private-sector workers. As with the data on current job patterns, this suggests that civil-service workers could hold positions in the private sector but choose not to.

Civil-Service Compensation and Personnel Policies

The main reason civil servants choose not to work in the private sector is that they find civil-service work more rewarding. However, these rewards do not necessarily mean the level of pay. Wages in the civil service are generally below those in the private sector for comparable occupations; however, health care coverage, retirement benefits, paid vacation, and regular working hours are more prevalent in the civil service.

For civil-service workers in these environments, the current private-sector wage premium is not enough to offset the value of civil-service benefits. An even greater wage premium or an increase in the relative generosity of private-sector benefits would provide incentives for these workers to consider private-sector employment more strongly.

Recommendations for Changing Civil-Service Compensation and Personnel Policies

The KRG has some options for changing policies that will decrease the relative desirability of civil-service employment. Each of these has advantages and disadvantages, so the specific mix of policies must be chosen with care. Furthermore, some strategies that help with downsizing in the near term could adversely affect longer-term reform:

- Develop a strategic human resource plan to ensure that short-term policies are consistent with the KRG's long-term goals.
- Establish a civil-service management agency with jurisdiction over all relevant personnel policies.

The KRG can take several steps to reduce civil-service employment:

- Impose a temporary hiring freeze in occupations that are not inherently governmental.
- Limit government hiring substantially while still ensuring that essential positions are filled.
- Reduce the financial benefits of civil-service employment.
- Slow the pace of civil-service promotions by increasing the number of years before a worker is considered for promotion, with exceptions for the highest performers.
- Promote only a fraction of eligible civil-service workers.

To hire qualified workers and promote workers based on performance, the KRG will need to make further reforms in its personnel management system. These actions include the following:

- Design and institute an appraisal system to measure and evaluate performance systematically.
- Develop career paths for civil-service workers in order to define worker expectations against which their performance can be measured.
- Develop written job descriptions for all occupations in the civil service.
- Strengthen the link between performance and promotion by awarding promotions only to the highest performers.
- Advertise all vacant positions openly as a way of finding qualified applicants, and hire the most-qualified applicants into each position.

Inducing Voluntary Separations from the Civil Service

Another option for altering the mix of civil-service and private-sector employment is to offer incentives that encourage civil-service workers to leave voluntarily. This option has two advantages. First, voluntary separations minimize the political costs associated with involuntary separations. Second, programs can be targeted to specific civil-service workers, helping the government keep its best performers and separate its worst.

Although such programs have worked elsewhere, it is not clear how well they will work in the KRI. In addition, the programs are costly, and workers who leave might attempt to return to government employment, negating the effects of the program. Therefore, careful design is essential, as is room for experimentation and adjustment.

Recommendations for a Voluntary Separation Program

Effective voluntary separation programs are those that are offered only to workers whom the government wants to leave. In addition, a flexible program allows policymakers to adjust separation incentives to ensure that the right number and types of worker separate:

- The KRG should design a voluntary separation program that is both *targeted* and *flexible*. A performance appraisal system will help officials choose the workers to be targeted.
- Target the program to civil-service workers in occupations that are not inherently governmental and to excess, low-productivity workers in any occupation.
- Prohibit workers who accept severance packages from returning to civil-service employment for a specific period of time.
- But be prepared to grant exceptions to this rule based on a clear set of criteria that includes a demonstrated need for specific skills or leadership abilities.
- Pilot test the program in a few ministries, adjust it as necessary, and then implement it throughout the KRG.

Most of the workers who leave the government will still need to find jobs in the private sector. The KRG should do the following:

- Work with the private sector to establish private sector–run clearinghouses for employers seeking workers and for civil-service workers seeking employment.
- Experiment with and support training and job placement programs, but evaluate them periodically to ensure that they are accomplishing their objectives.

The Need for Data Collection and Analysis

Many of our recommendations for both private-sector development and civil-service reform imply the need for data collection and analysis. In many of the areas on which we have focused, the KRG does not have the data necessary for us to offer more-specific recommendations. Both data collection and analysis are necessary to ensure that the KRG maximizes the return on its investment in any of these recommendations.

CHAPTER THREE

Strategic Priorities for Improving Access to Quality Education in the Kurdistan Region—Iraq

In 2007, the KRG launched an ambitious reform of its K–12 education system. It introduced a new, more rigorous curriculum, made education compulsory through grade 9 instead of grade 6, and restructured the previous three levels of schools into basic (grades 1–9) and secondary (grades 10–12). It put policies in place to reduce the high rate at which students were being held back in the early grades, and it instituted two national exams. Teacher training was a part of the reform, and all new teachers are now required to hold bachelor's degrees. In the context of this sweeping transformation, in 2010, the KRG asked RAND to assess the current status of the K–12 system and recommend ways to increase KRI students' access to education and to improve quality.

RAND's overarching goal was to build on the recently instituted reform and help the KRG move rapidly toward high-quality, universal, basic education. In a one-year, multimethod study, we analyzed school data from the Ministry of Education and from other government sources in the KRI and Iraq; interviewed a wide variety of stakeholders, including staff from the Ministry of Education and teacher colleges, school principals, teachers, and school supervisors; surveyed teachers; reviewed the new K–12 curriculum and the curriculum used in the teacher colleges; developed a model to project future student enrollment; used GIS mapping to display the distribution of schools and assess the feasibility of proposed actions; and reviewed the literature on best practices and relevant educational policies.

Our analysis suggested three strategic priorities for the KRG to improve the K–12 system:

- Expand capacity to meet the rapidly growing demand for education.
- Improve the quality of instruction.
- Strengthen stakeholder incentives and accountability.

First Strategic Priority: Expand Capacity

The KRI's K–12 education system has grown quickly over the past five years: On average, 67,000 new students have enrolled annually. The net enrollment rate is nearly 100 percent in the primary grades. However, it is much lower in grades 7–9 (0.47) and 10–12 (0.22), and growth has been greater in those grades (averaging 4.9 and 13.8 percent per year, respectively).

School capacity has not kept up with this rapid growth. As a result, more than half of schools in the KRI have added one or more shifts or started sharing a building with another school. This is especially true in urban areas and in grades 7–12. Compounding the problem is the fact that schools in urban areas—both single- and double-shift alike—are often overcrowded, with an average class size of 42 students. In contrast, class size in rural areas averages 14 students.

This pressure on capacity is unlikely to diminish over the next decade and might even increase. By our projections, enrollment will grow annually by anywhere from a low of 69,000 to a high of 111,000 new students, depending on birth rates, the annual increase in the number of students who complete basic education, and the speed at which gender parity is attained. This growth means that the KRG will need to add the equivalent of 21,400 to 34,700 new classrooms in these ten years (assuming an average class size of 35 students). Tackling the problem of overcrowding in urban schools would require an additional 5,200 new classrooms.

A growing demand for new teachers also contributes to the capacity problem. To meet the projected growth in enrollment, the KRG will need to hire 4,800 to 6,900 additional teachers annually over the next decade. Teachers of Kurdish, mathematics, and science will be in greatest demand.

Build New Schools and Classrooms

To meet the demand for new school spaces and to reduce crowding in current schools, the KRG would need to build between 134 and 202 new 18-classroom schools every year until 2021 to both cover the growth in student numbers and reduce overcrowding. The capital investment required to build that many schools using traditional construction methods will range from $200 million to $300 million annually—much in excess of the KRG's current annual investment for this purpose. To reduce this investment by 15 to 30 percent, the KRG could use prefabricated schools. These schools offer the added advantage of taking only six to eight months to build, compared with the 18–24 months needed to build schools using traditional methods.

Should the KRG's capital resources be insufficient to build this many new schools, we recommend that it consider four strategies, mainly applicable in urban areas, for reducing the number of new schools required:

- Redistribute students from overcrowded to uncrowded schools.
- Lower the rate at which students are retained in primary grades (1–6).
- Add a second shift to all existing single-shift schools.
- Add a second shift to all newly built schools.

These measures would reduce the number of new schools to be built by as much as 60 percent. But a need would still remain for the equivalent of 50 to 85 new 18-classroom schools annually.

In rural areas, one promising way to reduce the need for new schools would be to consolidate all students in a particular catchment area into one large school rather than have them attend several small schools. Although the KRG would need to provide transportation for students whose homes are not within walking distance of the new consolidated school, economies of scale in the number of teachers and principals and better education should compensate for the added transportation costs.

Hire New Teachers

To meet the coming demand for new basic-school teachers, the teacher colleges will have to increase their annual output of graduates (currently about 1,000 per year) by four to five times (to 4,000–5,000). However, until they do, there is seemingly no shortage of potential teachers among the graduates of education and other academic programs at universities (including mathematics and science). The Ministry of Education can draw from these ranks to offset the shortage of needed graduates from the teacher colleges and to meet the demand for new secondary school teachers.

Second Strategic Priority: Improve the Quality of Instruction

Basic indicators of student achievement show that students in the KRI are performing poorly. In about two-thirds of urban schools, more than 50 percent of students failed the school's assessment in 2007–2008. More than two-thirds of Kurdish students have been retained at least one year by the time they reach grade 9. About one-third of ninth-grade students did not pass the national English, physics, and mathematics tests given in 2008–2009.

Three factors are contributing to these poor academic results. First, the ability of practicing teachers to teach the new curriculum is weak for a variety of reasons. Many teachers do not have the subject-matter knowledge required by the new curriculum. Some teachers are being compelled to teach subjects outside of their specialization. Teachers receive little on-the-job training. Most teachers do not possess a bachelor's degree. In addition, new teachers are not being sufficiently trained in teaching methods or given practical experience before being certified.

Second, KRI schools provide too little instructional time. Single-shift basic schools offer 693 hours of instruction per year; double-shift schools, 539 hours—both well below the OECD average of 794 hours. The amount of time spent in the classroom in grades 7–12 is also much less than in OECD countries. Moreover, the new curriculum was designed to be taught in the context of more instructional hours, and teachers say that they cannot cover it fully in the number of hours in the current school day.

A lack of challenging learning opportunities for Kurdish students who demonstrate above-average talents and particular promise is a third factor contributing to student underachievement in the KRI.

Improve Teacher Training for Both Practicing and New Teachers

Upgrade the Knowledge and Expertise of Practicing Teachers. We recommend that the KRG establish regional training centers, possibly associated with the teacher colleges. These centers should be staffed by professional, full-time trainers, who could be recruited from among the KRI's best supervisors and teachers. These recruits should be thoroughly trained on the new curriculum before beginning to train other teachers. Detailed standardized training material should be developed for use in the centers to ensure that teacher training is taking place in a consistent manner across the KRI.

Initially, the training centers should focus on increasing the subject-matter knowledge of practicing teachers so that teachers can competently cover the content of the new curriculum. Training on teaching methods should eventually follow. Training should build on those methods most familiar to practicing teachers (such as lecturing, instead of the still too poorly defined student-centered methods) and focus on the most practical techniques for large classrooms. It is appropriate to provide content-related training before providing training on teaching methods: Studies have shown that knowledge of subject matter is more important for student learning than teaching methods are.

A second measure to better prepare practicing teachers is to develop "curriculum maps." These give teachers step-by-step guidance on how and what to teach, combining recommended content, suggestions for teaching methods and classroom exercises, student assessment, monitoring, and teaching plans. The maps (if teachers follow them) ensure that teachers present the curriculum in a standardized fashion.

A third set of measures would be to develop, over time, a support infrastructure that would assign expert mentors to teachers who may need them and to establish professional communities of teachers across schools to promote knowledge exchanges and better align the curriculum.

Upgrade the Preparation of New Teachers. The curriculum of the teacher colleges should be restructured, with the assistance of an outside teacher college. The aims should be to do the following:

- Increase the number of courses on teaching methods.
- Require one semester of experience as a teacher's aide.
- Require both a major and a minor specialization.
- Reflect more closely the content of the national basic curriculum.

University graduates recruited to become either basic or secondary teachers should also be required to take a course in teaching methods and acquire at least one semester of experience as a teacher's aide.

To attract highly qualified and motivated individuals into the teaching profession, the minimum score required on the 12th-grade exit exam for graduates to be assigned to the teacher career track should be raised. In addition, students who score high on the exit exam should not be automatically assigned to a nonteaching profession, as they are now. Those who express a desire to become a teacher should be allowed to enroll in a teacher college or university education program.

Increase Instructional Time

We recommend that the KRG expand the school year from 170 to 190 days and lengthen the shifts in double-shift schools from four to five hours. These changes would bring instructional time in KRI schools in line with international standards.

Provide High-Performing Students with Broadened Learning Opportunities

High-performing students should be identified using a transparent selection process and tracked in separate schools, entering in either the seventh or tenth grade. The program can start small but should aim to eventually offer entry to 10–15 percent of all KRI students.

Third Strategic Priority: Strengthen Stakeholder Accountability and Incentives

Accountability involves monitoring the performance of an education system; incentives motivate education leaders, principals, teachers, and parents to behave in ways that will improve student performance. At present, the KRI has a limited system for accountability and incentives, and some areas could be strengthened. For example, the current teacher evaluation system is based on a supervisory model. The Ministry of Education maintains 830 supervisors for basic education. During three school visits per year, they both evaluate and train teachers. Yet their evaluation criteria are not specific or consistent. Many do not have sufficient knowledge of a subject area or spend enough time in a given school to make judgments on the performance of either the school or individual teachers. The fact that supervisors are asked to perform a dual role as both evaluator *and* trainer creates a potential conflict of interest.

Decisionmaking is centralized in the Ministry of Education. Principals receive no data from the ministry that would allow them to compare their students' performance with that of students in other schools or track trends in their schools' performance over time. Principals also have limited input into teacher evaluation and no say in the assignment of teachers to their schools. Indeed, their role is mainly administrative: They are not expected to be instructional leaders.

Finally, parental and public participation in the KRI education system is minimal.

Restructure the Role of Supervisors

The role of supervisors should be limited to monitoring and evaluating the performance of schools and teachers. This change should be carried out in tandem with the professionalization of teacher trainers.

Redesign the System for Evaluating Teacher Performance

The evaluation criteria should be aligned with the new curriculum. More objective measures, including student performance, should also be used to draw conclusions about how well teachers are performing in the classroom.

Increase the Role of the Principal

Currently, the principal's input into a teacher's evaluation is worth only 25 percent of the total score. We recommend raising this share to 50 or even 75 percent. Over time, principals should also be given more authority over the assignment, hiring, and firing of teachers.

Reward High-Performing Schools

Recognition should be used to incentivize schools to perform in accordance with high standards.

Measure Student Achievement and Progress, and Make Results Public

The KRG should continue to use the annual national exams at grades 6, 8, and 9 to measure educational progress. This information should then be made available to principals, teachers, and parents. We also recommend participation in one of the international assessments of student achievement so that the KRG can benchmark the performance of KRI students with that of students in other countries.

Involve Parents and the Public in Promoting Education

A process should be established to enable parents and the public to consult with principals, teachers, and other key stakeholders. In this way, they can be included in decisionmaking about educational improvements.

Implementing the Recommendations

The effort involved in implementing our recommended changes may, at first, seem daunting; however, they need not all be implemented at once. Our vision is that the Ministry of Education would put these recommendations into action over multiple years, in part to avoid overloading principals and teachers with too many changes at the same time and in part to manage the sheer scale of the effort that will be involved.

To make the process manageable, we recommend a coordinated, three-pronged approach to implementing our recommendations:

- Use task forces for each primary recommendation to make key decisions; design new policies, programs, and operational guidelines; and develop detailed implementation plans.
- Conduct implementation in phases.
- Coordinate those parts of implementation that affect all the task forces equally.

CHAPTER FOUR

The Future of Health Care in the Kurdistan Region—Iraq

The KRG asked RAND to analyze the current health care system in the KRI; to make recommendations for better using resources to improve the quality, access, effectiveness, and efficiency of primary care; and to define the issues entailed in revising the existing health care financing system.

RAND staff reviewed available literature on the KRI and its health care system, as well as information relevant to primary care. We interviewed a wide array of policy leaders, health practitioners, patients, and government officials to gather information and understand their priorities, and we collected and studied all available data related to health resources, services, and conditions.

Using the available information, we described current service utilization, projected demand for services five and ten years into the future, and calculated the additional resources (e.g., beds, physicians, nurses) needed to meet future demand. We used these data, as well as information from those we interviewed, to develop an array of options for improving primary care organization and management, the health workforce, and information systems and to address issues in health financing. We developed an extensive list of policy options, discussed them with key policy leaders in the Kurdistan Region and among the research team to rate options by importance and feasibility, and then used the criteria to identify a subset of policy changes as potentially the highest priority for implementation over the next two years.

Summary Assessment of the Current Kurdistan Region—Iraq Health System

The health system in the KRI has many strengths:

- Access to care is excellent. The majority of people live within 30 minutes of some type of a primary health care center (PHC); in remote regions, hospital and emergency services are increasingly accessible.
- The total number of health facilities is adequate. All governorates have public general, emergency, and pediatric hospitals, and most PHCs provide most of the basic primary care services.
- Health care providers are knowledgeable and strongly committed to patient health.
- The commitment of health system leaders is strong, and they have set appropriate strategic goals and priorities for improvement.

However, the primary care health system also faces challenges:

- The overall distribution of PHCs and medical staff is not optimal. Slightly fewer than 30 percent of the 847 PHCs have at least one physician. Services offered at each type of facility and reporting requirements are not standardized. Facilities are not systematically networked, referrals are not well organized.
- The quality and availability of primary care vary. Quality is not systematically measured, and most personnel lack training in quality improvement methods.
- Physicians are overworked; nurses are underutilized and lack appropriate training. The number and distribution of medical staff are not optimal, especially in rural areas. Many general practitioners in PHCs are neither supervised nor mentored, and many physicians work only in the morning, devoting the rest of the day to private practice. Job descriptions and staff performance standards are lacking, and few health care managers are trained.
- Health information systems are not systematically used to support policymaking, regulation, or system management. Data collection and analysis are not standardized, and computer technologies are not fully utilized. Data systems are inefficient, and data are not readily available; available data are not routinely used at all relevant levels. Patient recordkeeping at ambulatory centers is virtually nonexistent.
- Health care is generally financed by government budgets with no incentives for efficiency. There is little private insurance.

A primary care–oriented health care system could help the KRG address many of these challenges. An ideal model is an integrated health care system that offers services at the appropriate level of care; creates incentives for patients to seek urgent and other care in the community, when appropriate; and integrates health information across levels of care. Such systems produce consistently higher-quality care and better clinical outcomes, with associated lower costs.

Projecting Future Health Care Supply and Utilization for the Kurdistan Region

To estimate future resource needs, we projected future demand and supply for health services in the KRI under a variety of assumptions. In the base case, we projected changes in utilization that would occur in the future as a result of current population growth, with all other parameters of care held constant. We then changed these assumptions in some scenarios to compare the gap between supply and needs under different scenarios.

Estimating Future Demand for Health Care: Base Case

We first projected health care supply and utilization for 2015 and 2020, assuming moderate population growth consistent with recent levels of population growth in the Kurdistan Region (3 percent annual growth between 2010 and 2020) and unchanged patterns of health service delivery and utilization. Table 4.1 shows additional workforce and hospital bed needs under these conditions.

Table 4.1
Projected Workforce and Hospital Bed Needs,
Base Case

Health Care Resources	2015	2020
Hospital beds	+1,343	+2,574
Physicians	+1,070	+2,097
Nurses	+1,681	+3,325
Dentists	+126	+246
Pharmacists	+82	+151

Estimating Demand for Health Care: Three Future Scenarios

We then estimated how the additional resources needed would change under different assumptions, focusing on three indicators of future health service utilization for each governorate: (1) total hospital admissions, (2) total emergency department visits, and (3) total outpatient visits (see Table 4.2).

Scenario 1 assumed rapid population growth due to expansion of the oil economy, with approximately a 2.4-percent yearly influx of foreign workers, primarily young male adults. The increase in net migration would result in an average annual population growth rate of 4.8 percent between 2010 and 2020 and a total projected population of about 8.75 million by 2020. These foreign workers will most likely be dominated by young males, who, in other countries, have higher rates of hospitalization and emergency department use and lower rates of outpatient care utilization. Under this scenario, hospitalizations could increase by as much as 28 percent over the base case by 2020, emergency department use by as much as 74 percent, and outpatient visits by as much as 8 percent.

Scenario 2 assumed enhanced primary care; fewer hospitalizations for care that could be provided in ambulatory facilities; increased outpatient utilization; and decreased emergency department utilization. These assumptions resulted in a 20-percent reduction in hospitalizations for chronic disease (a subset of overall hospitalizations), a 20-percent increase in outpatient visits, and a 20-percent decrease in emergency department utilization.

Scenario 3 assumed expansion of the private health care sector. These assumptions result in broad increases in utilization (2–10 percent in inpatient utilization, 5–20 percent in outpatient utilization, no change in use of emergency care).

Table 4.2
Summary of Projected Changes in Resource Requirements in 2020 for Each Scenario, Compared with the Base Case (% difference)

Scenario	Hospitalizations	Emergency Department Visits	Outpatient Visits
Rapid population growth	28	75	8
Improved primary care (lower-bound estimate)	−1	−20	20
Growth in private-sector health care	2–10	0	5–20

Health Care Financing System

The KRG's Minister of Planning asked RAND to review the basic tenets of health care financing and to develop a road map to help guide KRG policy development in this area. We (1) provided an overview of health care financing and its basic tenets, (2) examined how other countries have dealt with financing issues, (3) developed a general profile of Kurdistan's present health care financing system, and (4) defined the questions the KRG will need to address as it considers its future financing system.

A country's health care financing system enables equitable collection of sufficient resources to offer efficient, quality care to all segments of society. The system defines the compensation that providers will receive and embodies incentives that help determine efficiency and quality of care. The system also reflects a country's basic cultural and economic values.

No two countries finance health care exactly the same way because each country has its own objectives, cultural context, and health status. But every health financing system must determine who is eligible for health care coverage, what services will be covered, where the funds will come from to pay for services, how the funds will be pooled, and how payment for services will be made.

Most financing systems fall into one of the five general types of health financing systems shown in Figure 4.1. The type of system a country has depends on a range of factors, including data systems, ability to collect taxes, the public workforce, number of physicians, education of the population, and the sophistication of the banking and insurance systems. Almost all countries have mixed systems.

Kurdistan's current health care financing system is primarily a public budget system. All Iraqis are covered under the system, and a wide range of primary, hospital, and other medical care is offered in the public facilities, where most health care is provided. Some services are provided by private hospitals and physicians in private practice.

Most services are paid for out of public budgets (KRG, governorates, or Baghdad); private physician and hospital services are paid for by individuals. In theory, the government regu-

Figure 4.1
Common Health Care Financing Systems

Private ◄─────────	Public ──────────►			
Private pay	**Public budget**	**Private health insurance**	**Social health insurance**	**National health service**
• **Main revenue type:** personal	• **Main revenue type:** public budgets	• **Main revenue type:** individual and employer payments	• **Main revenue type:** payroll tax, government budget	• **Main revenue type:** general taxes
• **Pooling:** none	• **Pooling:** government	• **Pooling:** privately managed pools	• **Pooling:** pools by job or income	• **Pooling:** national pool
• **Purchasing:** individual	• **Purchasing:** by government	• **Purchasing:** selective contracts	• **Purchasing:** collective and selective contracts	• **Purchasing:** national or regional direct purchase of services it provides

lates both the public and private health care sectors. Private insurance is almost nonexistent. Copayments for public services are very low. Costs are rising quickly, as are payments for care abroad. The system provides few incentives for efficiency, quality, or cost control.

The Kurdistan Region currently lacks the sophisticated data, information technology (IT) systems, and managerial skills required to successfully operate more management-intensive systems, such as social insurance or national health plans. These requirements must be in place before the KRG can successfully embark on reform. However, the KRI is rapidly developing and will likely be able to take the next step in establishing systems that are not primarily budget-driven. Careful planning and wise choices can help the Kurdistan Region achieve the health outcomes of much richer countries at a greatly reduced cost.

To examine other finance system options, the KRG will need to address multiple dimensions of the five key issues: eligibility, coverage, sources of funds, pooling of funds, and payment. The KRG also needs to begin a systematic review of all policy options and choices, including (1) what data are required to manage any system, (2) what actions can be taken now to improve efficiency and control costs, and (3) what incentives should be embedded in the system to ensure quality health care for all KRI residents. The KRG will also need a strategic health care financing plan and a research agenda to fulfill it.

Improving Primary Care

Primary care is key to the success of a modern health care system. Primary care serves as an anchor for the organization of health services by providing an ongoing patient-clinician connection for delivery of most care and a pathway to and from other sources of care. The Minister of Health and other KRG authorities identified improving primary care as a high priority. To address this priority, we examined the organization and management of primary care and associated needs related to the health workforce and health information systems.

Following our analysis of the current system, discussions with health care leaders and managers throughout the region, and guiding principles of primary care in the 21st century, we offered recommendations for improving Kurdistan's primary care system in three areas: (1) organization and management of primary care facilities and services, (2) the health care workforce, and (3) health information systems.

Organization and Management of Primary Care Facilities and Services

The KRI's primary health care system has important strengths on which to build, but it also faces challenges. We focus on three key goals for improving the organization and management of primary care facilities and services: (1) distribute facilities and services efficiently, (2) develop and implement a system for referrals and continuity of care, and (3) develop and implement a program for continuous quality improvement (CQI).

Distribute Facilities and Services Efficiently. The types, sizes, and locations of hospitals are relatively standardized across the three provinces. However, the PHCs are much less standardized, and the number of main PHCs (staffed by a physician) on a per capita basis falls short of international and Iraqi standards. Iraqi law defines different types of health centers and establishes criteria for population covered, physical infrastructure, and staffing at each type of facility, but these criteria have not been applied consistently across the region.

Functionally, the KRI primary care system has two types of centers:

- *PHC main center* (categories A, B, and C): Serving a population of 5,000 to 10,000, these are staffed with at least one physician, and they deliver all primary care services. Type B centers also serve as medical and paramedical training centers, and type C centers provide uncomplicated obstetric deliveries and simple medical and surgical emergency care.
- *PHC subcenter or branch* (category D): Serving a population up to 5,000, these are staffed by a male nurse, a female nurse, and a paramedical assistant. They provide simple maternal and child health services, immunizations, and simple curative services.

Health authorities suggest that PHCs are not necessarily distributed appropriately in the region, nor are they systematically standardized or monitored by such criteria as type, size of population served, staffing level, and services offered. Experts have also argued persuasively that chronic disease management should now be included in the package of primary care services because nearly three-fourths of avoidable mortality—including a significant proportion of deaths in the Kurdistan Region—can be attributed to behavioral and environmental factors, such as poor diet, lack of exercise, tobacco use, and alcohol consumption. Each of these can be significantly reduced through public education and other prevention-oriented interventions.

An important goal in the Kurdistan Region should be to make primary care services more comprehensive and more uniformly and universally accessible at appropriate levels of care. Absence of functional KRG standards for catchment areas, staffing, and services hampers efficiency and systematic improvement. The goals of universal access and high-quality care cannot be achieved without systematic application of such standards. Making the scope of services more uniform at each level of care is also a prerequisite to improving service quality, efficiency, and staff productivity.

We recommend that immediate attention be given to aligning services with appropriate levels of care, ensuring that facilities are properly equipped and staffed and can provide all appropriate services, and ensuring the quality of those services.

We suggest six specific strategies for achieving efficient distribution of facilities and services while maintaining sufficient flexibility to reflect different local conditions: (1) *Define the appropriate scope of services to be provided at public-sector clinics*, (2) *organize the system of existing and new PHCs based on a core three-tiered networked system and specified access standards*, (3) develop a plan to provide services based on standards appropriate for each type of facility, (4) extend the reach and quality of health services through telemedicine, (5) expand health education activities in clinics and schools, and (6) develop and implement public health education campaigns to promote safe and healthy behaviors of greatest relevance to the region.

The first two strategies (italicized above) seem the most important and feasible in the near term.

Develop and Implement a System for Referrals and Continuity of Care. If a primary care facility cannot provide specific services that are needed (e.g., specialized diagnostic or surgical care), continuity of care requires efficient referral from and back to a patient's first-level health facility. Ideally, there would be no gaps in care due to lost information or failed communication between providers. A patient should have a regular point of entry into the health system and an ongoing relationship with his or her primary care team. Continuity of care is also essential in chronic disease management, reproductive health, mental health, and healthy child development and requires that the system be as easy as possible for patients to use.

A system for referrals and continuity of care aims to ensure that patients receive services at the most appropriate time and in the most appropriate setting and that care is well coordinated across care levels and providers and entails no inappropriate delays or interruptions. The KRI does not currently have such a system.

We offer four specific interventions to improve referrals and continuity of care, of which the first appears to be the most important and at least moderately feasible to implement: (1) *Develop and implement a patient referral system*, (2) explore the feasibility of designating population catchment areas and a "home clinic" and primary care provider for all population members, (3) begin transitioning to electronic health records at all levels to facilitate referrals and continuity of care, and (4) promote local awareness of available services, appropriate use, and referrals within and beyond the local catchment area.

Develop and Implement a Program for Continuous Quality Improvement. The Kurdistan Region currently lacks a program to assess quality of care, draw lessons from any issues identified, or institute appropriate changes or incentives within the system to promote quality. These activities are the heart of CQI, an essential component of effective care. The goal of CQI is to help health systems and professionals consistently improve the quality of health care delivery and outcomes through access to effective knowledge and tools. An essential requirement for CQI is establishing clinical practice standards that are uniform and based on best evidence.

We suggest six specific interventions focused on CQI: (1) *Develop and implement evidence-based clinical management protocols for common conditions seen at ambulatory and hospital facilities*, (2) *define and expand the safe scope of practice for nurses in ambulatory settings*, (3) adopt standardized patient encounter forms (e.g., checklists) to facilitate use of clinical management protocols at PHC facilities at all levels, (4) identify and test efficiency measures to enhance patient flow, (5) develop and implement carefully focused surveys of client and staff satisfaction on a routine basis at PHC facilities, and (6) explore the feasibility of a regional and, ultimately, international accreditation process for ambulatory and hospital inpatient services.

In the near term, the first two interventions (italicized above) appear to be the most important and at least moderately feasible.

The Health Workforce

Many studies have demonstrated that the size and qualifications of a country's health workforce affect health outcomes. Preparing the workforce requires both careful planning and strategic investments in education, all designed to address the country's key health system priorities. Once trained, the workforce needs to be properly managed—clinical skills monitored, maintained, and updated.

Iraq has a long tradition of excellence in medical services and training. But areas for improvement remain with regard to the numbers and qualifications of its health workforce. For example, the Kurdistan Region has fewer physicians per capita than many other countries in the region. Physician shortages involve training and competencies, as well as numbers, distribution (shortages are especially pronounced in rural areas), and hours worked. Public-sector ambulatory care relies almost exclusively on obligatory one-year service of junior general practice physicians who have completed one or two years of postgraduate clinical (residency) training and who return afterward for a final year of residency training in which they can begin to specialize.

During the final residency year, these physicians receive no mentorship, supervision, or other professional development support, and they have limited access to professional resources, such as the Internet or professional journals. Virtually all of them provide clinic services in the morning and see private patients in the afternoon. All physicians who have completed their clinical training have guaranteed government jobs (and pensions), but they receive relatively meager government salaries for public-sector work and derive much more substantial income from seeing private patients.

According to KRG health authorities and consistent with our own observations, problems with the nursing profession are especially critical. The KRI has more nurses per capita than some countries in the region and fewer than others. However, the Minister of Health has indicated that the *number* of nurses in Kurdistan may not be as important as the *distribution*, *qualifications*, and *competencies* of nurses across all levels. The Minister of Health and most other health authorities are particularly concerned about poor quality of nursing care; lack of defined nursing competencies, responsibilities, and duties; and the resulting inefficient use of nurses in clinical care.

We focus on two goals for improving the health workforce in Kurdistan: (1) enhancing professional qualifications through education and training and (2) improving the distribution and performance of the health workforce through specific human resource management interventions.

Enhance Professional Qualifications Through Education and Training. The number and quality of health workers demonstrably affect all health outcomes, and the decisions they make determine whether resources are used efficiently and effectively. The U.S. Institute of Medicine recommends education that includes practical experiences so that clinicians master five specified core competencies: (1) patient-centered care, (2) ability to work in interdisciplinary teams, (3) utilization of evidence-based practice, (4) application of quality improvement, and (5) utilization of informatics.[1]

We offer 11 specific strategies to improve professional education and training: (1) *Establish an executive committee to develop and oversee new professional education, training, licensing and recertification standards, recruitment of students across the medical professions, and management of the supply of medical personnel to meet forecasted demand*; (2) *preferentially recruit medical and nursing students from rural areas to attract professionals to more permanent rural service*; (3) *include primary care in medical and nursing school curricula*; (4) *provide preferential incentives and professional development opportunities to general-practice physicians during their year of obligatory medical service*; (5) enhance the profile of family medicine; (6) include primary care in the clinical rotations of medical and nursing schools; (7) enhance training in practical clinical skills throughout all the phases of medical and nursing preparation; (8) revise and implement new nursing curricula and training at nursing schools; (9) develop and implement a mandatory continuing education system for medical, nursing, dental, and pharmacy professionals; (10) develop and implement a system for licensing and revalidation for medical professionals; and (11) enhance training and create a strong career track for preventive-medicine specialists.

The first four strategies (italicized above) might be the most appropriate near-term priorities because of their relative importance and feasibility.

Enhance the Distribution and Performance of the Health Workforce. Recruiting and retaining health care workers, especially in remote and rural areas, is not a problem unique to Kurdistan. It is seen worldwide and has been a focus of considerable research effort. WHO has

---

[1] Institute of Medicine, "Quality Through Collaboration—The Future of Rural Health," Washington, D.C.: National Academy Press, 2005.

identified two types of factors that influence the choices of doctors, nurses, and midwives to work in rural areas. Factors that attract workers include better employment or career opportunities, better income and allowances, better living and working conditions, better supervision, and a more stimulating environment for worker and family. Factors that repel workers include job insecurity, poor working and living conditions, poor access to education for the workers' children, inadequate availability of employment for the workers' spouses, and work overload.

We offer six specific interventions to help improve health workforce management: (1) *Develop, implement, and monitor qualifications and job descriptions for professional staff at all relevant levels*; (2) develop a plan to distribute staff based on standards defined by law for each type of facility; (3) provide supportive supervision for physicians, nurses, and other health professionals serving in PHCs, especially in rural and remote areas; (4) institute appropriate incentives to attract medical, dental, and nursing staff to serve (and remain) in rural and remote areas; (5) increase the use of online human resource management forms, including applications for study, training, placement, licensure, continuing education, and related documentation; and (6) develop and implement strategies to reduce fraudulent private medical practice.

The first strategy (italicized above) appears to be both important and feasible in the near term.

Health Information Systems

A health care system depends on data to guide wise investments in policies and programs and to monitor their implementation. Management information systems make it possible to monitor health resources, services, and clinic utilization. Surveillance and response systems support the monitoring of mortality, morbidity, and health risk factors. Implementing such systems requires trained personnel and standardized data collection, processing, analysis, and presentation. Patient recordkeeping is key to managing primary care facilities and underpins efficient referrals and continuity of care.

KRG policymakers wish to have such data, but a "culture of data for action"—in which data collection, processing, analysis, presentation, and use are routine and relatively easy—remains elusive. We focus on strategies to achieve two main goals, corresponding to two broad types of health information system: (1) Develop and implement health management information systems and (2) enhance surveillance and response systems.

Both of these critical systems serve managers at the regional, governorate, and district levels; improvements are highly feasible in the near term because the important foundations are already in place. A third type of data system—patient clinical recordkeeping—serves primarily clinical providers and patients. It is also critically important to primary care, but the foundations are not yet in place for this. Efforts to lay such foundations should be a near-term priority.

Develop and Implement Health Management Information Systems. Health management information systems include data on health resources, services provided, and service utilization. Management information systems can help ensure service coverage, performance, and efficiency. For example, these systems can help managers and policymakers track the proportion of the population that has access to health services within specified standards and determine whether the distribution of health facilities and services is adequate; monitor the services delivered at specific health facilities and the number and qualifications of health workers providing the services; track equipment and supplies at health facilities, utilization of health services, the percentage of the target population covered by each type of service, and the efficient use of health facility staff; determine the proportion of the intended population that receives preventive services; and monitor patient referrals and continuity of care across different levels and providers of health services.

We offer two main recommendations for enhancing health system monitoring: (1) *Develop a systematic mechanism to monitor clinic resources and services* and (2) *monitor clinic utilization.*

The first recommendation appears to be most important and feasible in the near term. Monitoring clinic utilization also seems critical and only slightly more difficult. Both would significantly enhance management and, ultimately, the efficiency and effectiveness of primary health care services.

Enhance Surveillance and Response Systems. Public health surveillance is the ongoing, systematic collection and dissemination of health-related data to be used for public health action and ongoing management. These data include mortality, morbidity, and risk factors for communicable diseases, noncommunicable diseases, and injuries. Surveillance systems should have broad and representative coverage and provide high-quality and timely data. Such systems make it possible to monitor trends in health outcomes and risk factors, detect unusual health events, and respond appropriately to anomalous events or trends.

Taking responsible action based on surveillance requires information collection designed to be actionable, adequate workforce numbers and analytic capabilities (particularly in the areas of applied epidemiology and statistics), and established response mechanisms and procedures (especially for epidemiologic investigation of outbreaks, implementation of appropriate control measures, and design of further research).

We offer ten strategies to improve KRG surveillance and response systems: (1) *Standardize the diseases and conditions to be included in routine surveillance,* (2) *standardize the data-collection forms,* (3) hire and train personnel who are responsible for specific surveillance functions, (4) conduct a systematic assessment of current surveillance systems at all levels, (5) standardize the sources of surveillance information and reporting processes, (6) streamline data processing at governorate and regional levels, (7) develop and disseminate standardized analyses for surveillance information, (8) develop and implement a system for immediate alerts, (9) develop and implement standardized protocols for responding to events warranting timely investigation, and (10) monitor health risk factors.

These strategies largely represent a logical progression for improving surveillance and response. However, near-term priorities might focus on the first two strategies (italicized above), which we judged to be both most important and most feasible.

Looking to the Future

The KRG has made significant progress in improving the region's health care services and the health of its people. However, more can be done, especially with respect to improving the health care system's quality, efficiency, organization, management, workforce, and data systems. Such initiatives will be increasingly important as Kurdistan continues on its trajectory of modernization and becomes more closely integrated with the rest of the world.

CHAPTER FIVE

Developing a System for Collecting Policy-Relevant Data for the Kurdistan Region—Iraq

Comprehensive and reliable statistics are essential for policy formulation in any region or country. Statistics make it possible to identify the most pressing needs, track the progress of policies and initiatives currently in place, and plan future development. Most important, statistics form the foundation upon which successful policy planning in many areas rests. The KRI is hampered by the lack of such statistics as it aims to improve infrastructure, encourage private-sector development, attract foreign investment, and create a sustainable economy.

The overall objectives of this project were to survey the availability of reliable policy-relevant data in the KRI, identify the high-priority areas for which the KRG requires data, and develop guidance for a system to collect these data on an ongoing basis.

We begin our discussion by describing the baseline conditions for data collection and statistics in the KRG, specifically current statistical institutions and available data and statistics. We then report on KRG policy priorities, the heart of our analysis. Because the KRG's goal is to have data-driven policy development, policy priorities should govern data collection. Given the policy priorities, we define the data indicators needed for each policy area, dividing them into critical indicators needed at the highest level of policymaking, high-priority indicators, and lower-priority indicators. We discuss how to reform and develop the KRG statistical system, focusing on data collection and handling methodologies and statistical institutions. We conclude by laying out a road map for reform.

Kurdistan Regional Government Statistical Institutions

The KRG's overall aim is to meet all of the central government's expectations regarding data collection but to exceed expectations on the amount and quality of data collected and the excellence of data-collection methodologies. The KRSO, which is responsible for supporting the statistical activities of the KRG, is located within the MOP. Among the MOP's objectives is preparing indicators for planning in cooperation with other units of the KRG and the private sector. The KRSO also houses the Department of Information and Mapping (DIM), which collects and analyzes data from GIS.

In addition to the MOP and the KRSO, every ministry has a statistical office, called either a statistics department or a planning department. These offices send their data upward within their respective ministries, although sometimes not systematically.

The KRSO is a natural repository of statistical information from other ministries and should lead the effort to upgrade the overall quality of KRG statistics. However, there is currently no legal authority granting the KRSO the mandate to collect statistics from or work with the various ministries, and the KRSO is not a formal recipient of such data at this time.

Available Data and Statistics

The KRG currently collects a large volume of data, but much of it is not usable or not available for policymaking, and there are major gaps. Perspectives on what constitutes "data" vary across organizations and individuals, making it difficult to identify existing data sources and data needs to inform decisionmaking.

Data-collection capacity and methods vary across government units. Storage methods also vary, with many agencies entering and storing data on paper, even when electronic means are available. In addition, awareness of data availability is poor: Staff members in one ministry often do not know what data other ministries collect.

There is a need to systematize and coordinate data-collection efforts, both within and across ministries. It is not clear that policymakers have timely access to data or an efficient system for identifying and using available data for decisionmaking. The KRG ministry websites are generally not good sources of data, and consistency across sites could be improved. Finally, there is little systematic data collection outside the government—for example, by universities or nonprofit organizations.

Despite these problems, the KRG has made promising progress toward collecting critical data to inform policy. The participation of the KRSO with the central government and the World Bank in the 2007 IHSES was a major accomplishment that has already provided policy-relevant data to help formulate policies to alleviate poverty. A key challenge will be to develop sufficient capacity within the KRSO so that the KRG need not rely primarily on multilateral agencies for large-scale data-collection efforts but can instead originate its own data collection to meet policy needs.

Policy Priorities of the Kurdistan Regional Government

To make the best use of data for policymaking, it is important to identify policy priorities and then identify the most supportive data indicators. Based on extensive discussions with numerous policymakers and a review of KRG documents, our interpretation of the overall policy goals of the KRG is as follows: (1) to develop a diversified economy that relies on the private sector and is not solely dependent on oil, (2) to support the economy and the well-being of the population with sufficient government and social services, and (3) to provide an education system and labor market opportunities that will improve the standard of living of the population.

Achieving these goals will be a multistage process. As a way to begin, we identified ten priority areas described in this section. We distinguish among short-to medium-term priorities aimed at satisfying the immediate needs of the KRI population; long-term, strategic priorities that aim to put the KRI on a stable path of growth and development; and collection of data that can be used across sectors and policies.

Five Essential Services for the Short and Medium Terms

A recurring theme we encountered among KRG policymakers is that certain services—specifically *health, education, water and sewerage, electricity,* and *roads and transportation*—are not only viewed as essential for the public but are also areas in which the public expects to see results from the government quickly. Given population growth, the demand for these services is increasing; nearly all officials we met mentioned effective provision of these services as top policy priorities.

Four Economic and Governance Issues for the Longer Term

Encouraging the *private sector* and reducing the government payroll is high on the list of KRG priorities, and instituting business-friendly reforms is a key item on the policy agenda. *Agriculture* is the sector most singled out for attention, followed by *tourism. Good governance and civil-service reform* is also a priority.

An Urgent Data Priority

A final priority related directly to data, specifically establishing *regional accounts* for the reporting of gross regional product. This would benefit from instituting regular household surveys to monitor labor market conditions and establishing regular agriculture and business surveys.

Data Requirements to Address Policy Priorities

We recommend collection of a comprehensive set of indicators to support policymaking in the priority areas. The indicators, which we have categorized as higher and lower priority, appear in a set of ten Excel spreadsheets that accompany the main report electronically. The complete set of indicators is unlikely to be necessary or even useful for top policymakers. Therefore, we have drawn from the larger list a smaller set of "critical indicators" for each sector—the indicators that should be the highest priority for collection and reporting to guide high-level policymaking in the KRG.

The complete set of indicators is intended solely to support policymaking. There has been some concern that the indicators might be used to evaluate the work of the ministries that generate them or that work in the relevant policy areas. We strongly caution against this use. These indicators may comprise a subset of the data needed for evaluation; however, much more data are needed to evaluate ministry performance fairly.

The data indicator spreadsheets are a broad resource for the KRG to guide data-collection activities, but they are not exhaustive lists of all data that should be collected. The goal is to guide the KRSO's data-collection activities so that they yield policy-relevant information that will be broadly beneficial across ministries. Ministries may choose to collect additional data.

Table 5.1 shows the details contained in the data indicator spreadsheets.

Crosscutting Data-Collection Issues

Several common issues emerged from our development of the indicators for the ten priority areas:

- Data will have to come from different sources, including administrative data, surveys, and even units of the Iraqi central government.

Table 5.1
Summary of Entries in Data Spreadsheets

Variable	Description
Data item	Broad categories and subcategories of data, individual data items, and definitions where needed
Priority	High- or low-priority data
Unit	Natural unit for data item (e.g., Iraqi dinars for gross value of fixed assets)
Source of data	Where data will come from (e.g., administrative data, surveys, or other sources)
Potential data-collection organization	Typically, the KRSO, in collaboration with the relevant ministry, but other agencies as well
Levels at which data should be reported	At district, governorate, or regional level (desired level of aggregation)
Data-collection frequency	Ongoing collection (e.g., health indicators), quarterly, or annually

- Data will often be applicable across policy areas. For example, labor statistics and an index of industrial production are relevant for both macroeconomic (regional accounts) and private-sector indicators.
- Relevant ministries, in collaboration with the KRSO, would potentially be responsible for data collection. However, the KRSO has the methodological expertise and should lead the collection efforts.
- Broad collaboration is especially essential for household surveys, which typically cover multiple areas, such as health, education, and employment.
- Data not collected by the KRSO might be shared with the KRSO less frequently than they are collected.

Critical Indicators

Some of the indicators identified for the ten policy areas are necessary for top KRG officials to make high-level policy decisions. We denote these as critical indicators and suggest that they have the highest priority for collection and dissemination, not only to senior levels of the KRG but also to the public (Table 5.2). These indicators represent the information that the prime minister, the Council of Ministers, senior advisers of the prime minister and ministers, and other top-level units, such as the KRG Economic Council, should be able to consult when making strategic planning decisions in the KRI.

Data-Collection Methodologies

Identifying, gathering, and disseminating comprehensive, high-quality and policy-relevant data requires using appropriate data-collection methods and instituting procedures for ensuring quality along many dimensions. The major types of data used for policy and planning purposes include *administrative data*, *census data*, and *surveys*. Each of these data types has benefits and costs.

Table 5.2
Critical Indicators to Inform Policymaking

Indicator	Data-Collection Frequency
Agriculture	
Production of staple crops (wheat, rice)	Seasonal and annual
Production of high-value crops (grapes, pomegranate)	Seasonal and annual
Land in use for agricultural production	5–10 years
Water used for irrigation	Annual
Education	
Number of new schools completed during the year	Annual
Percentage of teachers trained during the year	Annual
Gross student enrollment in secondary education	Annual
Net student enrollment in secondary education	Annual
Completion rate in secondary education	Annual
Electricity	
Unit nameplate capacity	Annual
Unit feasible capacity	Annual
Peak demand (load)	Semiannual
Governance	
Code of conduct implemented (de jure)	Annual
Public access to laws	Annual
Public access to regulations	Annual
Time to start a business (domestic enterprise)	Annual
Health	
Infant mortality (0–11 months)	Annual
Number and density of physicians per 10,000 population	Annual
Density of hospital beds per 10,000 population	Annual
Percentage of districts meeting standards for number of main public health centers (1 per 10,000 population)	Annual
Percentage of districts meeting standards for number of branch public health centers (1 per 5,000 population)	Annual
DPT3: Percentage vaccination coverage among 1-year-olds (12–23 months) with three doses DPT	Annual
Macroeconomics	
Total government expenditures	Monthly
Personal expenditures on goods and services	Quarterly
Exports of goods	Quarterly

Table 5.2—Continued

Indicator	Data-Collection Frequency
Imports of goods	Quarterly
Unemployment rate	Quarterly
Consumer Price Index	Monthly
Private sector	
Number of enterprises by economic activity	Annual
Number of persons employed by economic activity	Quarterly
Foreign direct investment inflow	Quarterly
Fixed investment by firms	Quarterly
Mobile phones per 1,000 people	Annual
Internet users per 100 people	Annual
Tourism	
Arrivals by class of visitor (overnight, same day)	Daily
Average length of stay (all types of establishments)	Annual
Average expenditure per day	Monthly
Transportation	
Extent of paved roads	Annual
Passenger vehicles traveling between major cities	Annual
Goods transported by road (tons/hour)	Weekly
Injury collision	Annual
Water	
Surface water stocks	Annual
Flows of water from inland water resources to economy	Annual
Losses of water in distribution	Annual
Population using improved water sources	Annual

NOTE: DPT = diphtheria-pertussis-tetanus.

Administrative data comprise information that is collected by the government or other entities for their own purposes. These data generally reflect the administration of programs, policies, or services; the data are not collected from the entire population. In contrast, a census is a count of all members of a specific population, whether individuals or other entities. Examples include people, enterprises, housing units, or even livestock.

Survey data are collected only from a sample of the population of interest. Survey data are usually collected in a way that enables statistical inferences to be made about the whole population.

Using these types of mechanisms to collect comprehensive, policy-relevant data is a multi-step process. Getting the essential elements right will help ensure that the final data products are accurate and useful. These elements include designing data-gathering instruments and protocols, sampling for survey data collection, implementing data collection, ensuring quality during the collection process, storing and disseminating data, and protecting the confidentiality of human subjects.

A comprehensive and integrated statistical system includes all three types of data collection. Population and other censuses usually form the central pillar of the system; in the KRI, censuses of enterprises and other nonpopulation censuses are likely to be the system's core in the short to medium term.

Censuses support surveys by providing information about the population to be surveyed, statistical infrastructure, statistical capacity, and benchmarks, and census data are often used as auxiliary information for dividing members of the population into homogeneous subgroups. Survey data complement census data by providing detailed information on complex topics. Because censuses cannot practicably be repeated frequently, surveys provide intermediate statistical updates. Data from surveys and administrative records can also be used to check census coverage and content and to determine the size and direction of any errors. Similarly, data from administrative records can be used to check and evaluate results from surveys and censuses. Combining these data sources is also useful analytically—for instance, census data and administrative data can be combined with survey data to produce inferences about small geographic areas or subpopulations.

Table 5.3 shows how a comprehensive data-collection program can be linked to the data priorities of the KRG, as represented by the critical indicators.

Human Capital for Data Collection and Management

Key to creating a high-quality data-collection system is the development of a skilled workforce. Developing a workforce with the skills necessary to collect, manage, and disseminate data in the KRI will be challenging. The KRSO can acquire additional capacity by hiring private- or nonprofit-sector firms on a contract basis, working with international organizations that have data expertise, or hiring employees with existing skill sets. Hiring outside firms gives the KRG the flexibility to access specialty skills as needed. But it could lead to higher management costs for the KRG and lower-quality data products if contractors are not vetted or managed well. The alternative is to train existing ministry or KRSO staff to give them additional skills.

Integrating Data-Collection Methodologies into a Work Plan for the Kurdistan Region Statistics Office

We recommend that the KRSO take the following steps to improve its data-collection methods:

- Plan and oversee an integrated work program that includes censuses of agriculture and enterprises, conducted every five to ten years. Multitopic household, farm, and enterprise surveys should be conducted at shorter intervals. Annual or semiannual collection of administrative data should be organized.
- Adopt consistent geographic units for collecting and reporting statistics.
- Adopt common definitions, concepts, and classifications across different data sources, including administrative records.
- Adopt electronic data-collection methodologies and electronic recordkeeping, where possible.
- Adopt and disseminate quality guidelines for data collection and handling.

Table 5.3
Data-Collection Options for Critical Data Indicators

Critical Indicator	Administrative Data	Enterprise/ Agriculture Census	Household Survey	Enterprise/ Organization Survey	Agriculture Survey	Special-Purpose Survey
Agriculture						
Production of staple crops (wheat, rice)		x	x		x	
Production of high-value crops (grapes, pomegranate)		x	x		x	
Land in use for agricultural production		x	x		x	
Water used for irrigation		x	x		x	
Education						
Number of new schools completed during the year	x					
Percentage of teachers trained during the year	x			x		x
Gross student enrollment in secondary education	x		x			
Net student enrollment in secondary education	x		x			
Completion rate in secondary education	x		x			
Electricity						
Unit nameplate capacity	x					
Unit feasible capacity	x					
Peak demand (load)	x		x	x		
Governance						
Code of conduct implemented (de jure)	x			x		
Public access to laws	x		x	x		

Table 5.3—Continued

Critical Indicator	Administrative Data	Enterprise/Agriculture Census	Household Survey	Enterprise/Organization Survey	Agriculture Survey	Special-Purpose Survey
Public access to regulations	x		x	x		
Time to start a business (domestic enterprise)		x				x
Health						
Infant mortality (0–11 months)	x		x			
Number and density of physicians per 10,000 population	x	x				
Density of hospital beds per 10,000 population	x	x				
Percentage of districts meeting standards for number of main public health centers (1 per 10,000 population)	x			x		
Percentage of districts meeting standards for number of branch public health centers (1 per 5,000 population)	x			x		
DPT3: Percentage vaccination coverage among 1-year-olds (12–23 months) with three doses DPT	x		x			
Macroeconomics						
Total government expenditures	x					
Personal expenditures on goods and services			x			
Export of goods		x		x		
Import of goods		x		x		
Unemployment rate			x			
Consumer Price Index						x

Table 5.3—Continued

Critical Indicator	Administrative Data	Enterprise/ Agriculture Census	Household Survey	Enterprise/ Organization Survey	Agriculture Survey	Special-Purpose Survey
Private sector						
Number of enterprises by economic activity	X	X				
Number of persons employed by economic activity	S	X	X	X		
Foreign direct investment inflow				X		
Fixed investment by firms		X		X		
Mobile phones per 1,000 people			X	X		X
Internet users per 100 people			X	X		X
Tourism						
Arrivals by class of visitor (overnight, same day)	X					
Average length of stay (all types of establishments)				X		X
Average expenditure per day						X
Transportation						
Extent of paved roads	X					
Passenger vehicles traveling between major cities	X					
Goods transported by road (tons/hour)	X			X		
Injury collision	X					

Table 5.3—Continued

Critical Indicator	Administrative Data	Enterprise/ Agriculture Census	Household Survey	Enterprise/ Organization Survey	Agriculture Survey	Special-Purpose Survey
Water						
Surface water stocks	x					
Flows of water from inland water resources to economy	x				x	x
Losses of water in distribution	x					
Population using improved water sources			x			

- Adopt and disseminate protocols and procedures for cleaning and storing data sets, especially protocols and procedures for handling sensitive data.
- Help develop institutions to protect the rights and welfare of survey participants.
- Create an online repository of data sources, including complete documentation, to facilitate use and analysis of data. The repository should be publicly accessible, and it should be regularly maintained and updated.
- Systematically monitor how data are used in order to improve collection, dissemination, and service.

In tandem with this work plan, an essential part of successful data collection is a high-quality information and communications technology (ICT) infrastructure. To move toward this goal, the KRSO should coordinate closely with the Department of Information Technology (DoIT), which is currently designing and implementing an ICT strategy for the KRG.

Institutional Arrangements for Statistical Systems

As important as knowing what data to collect and how to collect them are the institutional arrangements of the statistics program. A data-collection system comprises the institutions, procedures, and mechanisms that interact with each other and the population in order to execute the statistical program. Actors in the system derive their authority from legislation defining their relationships. At a minimum, the legislation defines the statistical agency's authority to collect data, the nature of government oversight over the collection process, the structure of the agency responsible for data collection, the mechanism by which the agency's efforts are overseen, the expectations for agency capacity, and the agency's relationships with external and internal actors relevant to the execution of its mission.

The KRG has a unique opportunity to define its statistical system clearly through robust legislation that lays the foundation for the long-term development of a strong system of statistical collection and analysis. Passage of a statistics law should be among the KRG's highest priorities. Moreover, the KRG should institute technical and policy oversight boards. We also recommend that the KRG consider afresh whether the KRSO should be an office within the MOP or independent. There are valid arguments in both directions, and countries around the world do not follow a single practice. Transparency in collection and dissemination will be important to ensure data integrity.

Relations between the KRSO and the Iraqi Central Organization for Statistics and Information Technology (COSIT) will also be important. Various institutional arrangements are possible, including a formal council of the senior leadership of each organization. Because a core value of statistical systems is legitimacy and there is a need for public support for data-collection efforts, the KRSO rather than an agency of the federal Iraqi government is the appropriate organization to collect data within the KRI. However, these data must be comparable to data collected from the rest of Iraq. Comparability will add credibility to the KRI data and reduce uncertainty among users, signaling to a global audience the reliability and stability of the investment environment.

A Recommended Road Map to Policy-Relevant Data Collection

We have described the current status of data and data institutions in the KRG, recommended which indicators to collect and suggested the priority to assign to each, and highlighted institutional issues for ensuring a high-quality statistical system. Our recommendations can be implemented by following a step-by-step road map that reflects the time needed for each recommendation and the priority each recommendation should have in building a high-quality statistical system. The KRG should take the following steps:

- **Enact a statistics law.** A statistics law will formalize the organizational structure of the KRSO and its interactions with other KRG ministries and agencies, especially as they relate to data sharing. This law needs to be cognizant of the federal statistics law.
- **Convene stakeholder meetings.** The KRSO should convene a meeting of relevant policymakers to promote coordination and effective planning. This meeting can be used to communicate the KRSO's short- and medium-term plans, solicit feedback, cement cooperation in conducting surveys that cut across ministries, and get general buy-in from stakeholders.
- **Decide the composition of the policy and technical oversight boards.** We have recommended that the KRG institute a technical oversight board to advise the KRSO on matters of data-collection techniques and methodology, and a policy oversight board to ensure that KRSO's data-collection efforts focus on the KRG's policy priorities. Members of the technical oversight board could come from current and retired academics within the region and from the Kurdish diaspora; other researchers, including international researchers with expertise in the Kurdistan Region and data collection; and individuals from the private sector with technical expertise. Policy board candidates would include senior policymakers (typically at the level of general directors) from the ministries responsible for high-priority policy areas, high-level civil servants or policymakers from the individual governorates, and representatives from the Council of Ministers, the Parliament, and the DoIT.
- **Identify a data contact within each ministry.** The KRSO should work with the appropriate ministry in each of the priority policy areas to appoint a KRSO liaison who would be responsible for collecting the critical indicators and transmitting them to the KRSO at specified intervals.
- **Collect the critical indicators.** The relevant ministries should collect the critical indicators; however, the KRSO should monitor this process and provide technical assistance as needed. This is especially important given that most critical indicators are based on component data items that must be collected before the critical indicators can be calculated.
- **Implement the organograms.** The KRSO has developed organization charts (organograms) for reorganizing its offices in its headquarters and the three governorates. In the main report, we have provided a few recommendations for modifications, mainly to ensure consistency across the offices and with a draft statistics law. The organization charts need to be revised, and the modified structure should be implemented.
- **Improve human resources in the KRSO.** Our analysis identified several state-of-the art techniques and procedures that the KRSO should institute, as well as data-collection steps it must oversee. To implement these recommendations, the KRSO will need to recruit new staff and upgrade the qualifications of the current staff through training

courses and hands-on exercises. We recommend that the KRSO seek the services of outside experts to provide training courses and hands-on training to its staff, perhaps by jointly conducting a data-collection exercise, such as a survey. Alternatives include engaging high-quality foreign universities to design short courses to be given in Kurdistan or sending staff abroad for such courses.

- **Upgrade and install ICT Infrastructure.** To establish a centralized database and facilitate data sharing with the ministries, the KRSO requires a sophisticated ICT infrastructure. The KRSO should work with the DoIT and external IT consultants, as needed, to implement an ICT infrastructure in its headquarters and governorate offices. The KRSO should also give the ministries the requirements for data-sharing ICT infrastructure.

- **Decide whether to improve current indicators or collect new ones.** Several KRG agencies are currently collecting data components, including some of the data indicators we identified as high-priority in our spreadsheets. However, such efforts tend to be fragmented rather than part of a unified strategy. The KRSO needs to decide, in consultation with the relevant ministries, whether to improve collection of existing high-priority indicators or spend the resources on collecting indicators not currently collected, even if they are of a lower priority.

- **Collect the high-priority indicators.** The process of identifying data contacts within each ministry and collecting critical indicators will also pave the way for collecting indicators of a slightly lower priority. As with the critical indicators, data collection for priority indicators would be done by the relevant ministries. However, the KRSO would have to monitor this process and provide technical assistance as needed.

- **Conduct one-off surveys.** An annual household and business survey form the backbone of data-collection efforts (especially to get macroeconomic indicators) in many countries. However, conducting these surveys would require that the KRSO build sufficient capacity for these complex undertakings. The KRSO could begin by conducting one-off surveys—surveys designed to be conducted for a specified purpose—especially for specific districts or topics for which there is a high data need. Over time, these surveys could be converted to be regular and periodic.

- **Conduct routine surveys.** Conducting the above-mentioned one-off surveys will position the KRSO to conduct annual household and business surveys. In addition to providing macroeconomic information, these surveys will produce useful microlevel information. However, larger, routine surveys will require the cooperation of multiple ministries. Therefore, both the technical and the process experience that the KRSO will gain from the earlier steps would be useful here.

The road map steps will help the KRSO and the KRG to assemble the core elements of a quality data system. This, in turn, will increase the availability of data to help KRG leaders achieve their most important policy goals.

CHAPTER SIX

Summary and Conclusion

This compilation of the executive summaries of the four studies conducted for the KRG in 2010–2011 provides concrete steps to reform the KRG civil service and encourage private-sector employment, improve access to and the quality of education and primary health care, and design a transparent system to collect policy-relevant data, thereby allowing the KRG to more effectively achieve its goals.

In most cases, we have not recommended a single approach to improve these sectors, but rather have provided several strategies for both the short term and the longer term. Implementation of what we have recommended requires a well-articulated strategic plan for each area and a steady commitment on the part of policymakers to consistent execution, monitoring and evaluation, and continuous improvement. Some recommendations may require changes to laws, organizational realignment, or shifts in the mindset of policymakers.

Despite the different topics, these studies are related: A healthy, well-educated population can lead to a vibrant economy, data on which can aid the development of policies that promote further progress. We recommend that those who are interested in any given section read the detailed reports, which provide definitive recommendations and steps for improvement.

Over the past decade, the KRG has made great strides toward improving the social and economic well-being of the residents of the region. It is in a strong position to build on the progress made to date and to implement the suggested recommendations on institution building, data collection, and capacity building to move the region toward adopting the best practices followed around the world.